BIG PICTURE 📷 SPORTS

Meet the
GREEN BAY PACKERS

By
ZACK BURGESS

NORWOOD HOUSE 🏠 PRESS
CHICAGO, ILLINOIS

NorwoodHouse Press

P.O. Box 316598 • Chicago, Illinois 60631
For more information about Norwood House Press please visit our website at
www.norwoodhousepress.com or call 866-565-2900.

Photo Credits:
All photos courtesy of Associated Press, except for the following:
Black Book Archives (6, 7, 15, 18, 23), Philadelphia Chewing Gum Co. (10 top, 22),
Topps, Inc. (10 bottom, 11 top & bottom), The Upper Deck Co. (11 middle).

Cover Photo: Kevin Terrell/Associated Press

The football memorabilia photographed for this book is part of the authors' collection. The collectibles used
for artistic background purposes in this series were manufactured by many different card companies—
including Bowman, Donruss, Fleer, Leaf, O-Pee-Chee, Pacific, Panini America, Philadelphia Chewing Gum,
Pinnacle, Pro Line, Pro Set, Score, Topps, and Upper Deck—as well as several food brands, including
Crane's, Hostess, Kellogg's, McDonald's and Post.

Designer: Ron Jaffe
Series Editors: Mike Kennedy and Mark Stewart
Project Management: Black Book Partners, LLC.
Editorial Production: Lisa Walsh

LIBRARY OF CONGRESS CATALOGING-IN-PUBLICATION DATA
Names: Burgess, Zack.
Title: Meet the Green Bay Packers / by Zack Burgess.
Description: Chicago, Illinois : Norwood House Press, [2016] | Series: Big
    picture sports | Includes bibliographical references and index. |
    Audience: Grade: K to Grade 3.
Identifiers: LCCN 2015019579| ISBN 9781599537405 (Library Edition : alk.
    paper) | ISBN 9781603578431 (eBook)
Subjects: LCSH: Green Bay Packers (Football team)--Miscellanea--Juvenile
    literature.
Classification: LCC GV956.G7 B85 2016 | DDC 796.332/640977561--dc23
LC record available at http://lccn.loc.gov/2015019579

288N—072016
Manufactured in the United States of America in North Mankato, Minnesota

CONTENTS

Words in **bold type** are defined on page 24.

The Packers treat each other like family.

CALL ME A PACKER

Hard-working Green Bay, Wisconsin, is the smallest city to host a National Football League (NFL) team. The people there take great pride in their Packers. They always see a bit of themselves down on the field. The players see a little of themselves up in the stands, too.

In 1919, **Earl "Curly" Lambeau**  asked the Indian Packing Company for money to start a football team. That is how the Packers got their name. The team has had many great quarterbacks, including Brett Favre. They have led "The Pack" to 13 championships.

6

Brett Favre set many team passing records.

Packers fans love going to Lambeau Field on cold winter days.

BEST SEAT IN THE HOUSE

The Packers play their home games at Lambeau Field. It is one of the NFL's oldest and largest stadiums. Green Bay is one of the coldest cities in America. This gives the Packers a big home-field advantage.

SHOE BOX

The trading cards on these pages show some of the best Packers ever.

DON HUTSON

RECEIVER · 1935-1945

Don was the NFL's first superstar receiver. He created many of the passing plays teams use today.

RAY NITSCHKE

LINEBACKER · 1958-1972

Ray was a fearsome tackler and an excellent leader. The people of Green Bay named a bridge after him.

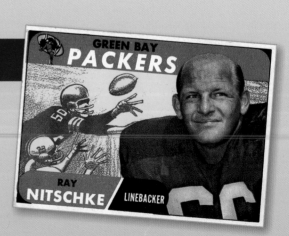

BART STARR

QUARTERBACK · 1956-1971

Bart led the Packers to five NFL championships. He was named Most Valuable Player (MVP) of the Super Bowl twice.

REGGIE WHITE

DEFENSIVE END · 1993-1998

Reggie was almost impossible to block. He had 68.5 **quarterback sacks** for the Packers.

BRETT FAVRE

QUARTERBACK · 1992-2007

Brett was a fearless passer who loved to win. He was named NFL MVP three years in a row.

THE BIG PICTURE

Look at the two photos on page 13. Both appear to be the same. But they are not. There are three differences. Can you spot them?

Answers on page 23.

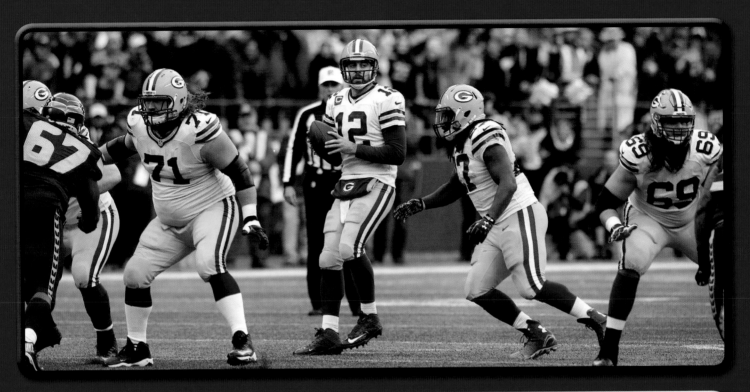

13

TRUE OR FALSE?

Aaron Rodgers was a star quarterback. Two of these facts about him are **TRUE**. One is **FALSE**. Do you know which is which?

1 Aaron has been named NFL MVP and Super Bowl MVP.

2 Aaron had a TV show called "Mr. Rodgers' Neighborhood."

3 Aaron began the 2008 season by throwing 157 passes without an **interception**.

Answer on page 23.

Aaron Rodgers warms up for a game.

15

It's not hard to find cheeseheads at a Packers game.

Go Packers, Go!

Wisconsin is known for its dairy products, including cheese. Fans in Green Bay are proud of this. They call themselves "cheeseheads." At Packers games, the stands are filled with fans wearing cheese-shaped hats on their heads!

ON THE MAP

Here is a look at where five Packers were born, along with a fun fact about each.

1 — **BUBBA FRANKS · RIVERSIDE, CALIFORNIA**
Bubba made the **Pro Bowl** three times for the Packers.

2 — **WILLIE DAVIS · LISBON, LOUISIANA**
Willie was the NFL's top defensive end in the 1960s.

3 — **CHARLES WOODSON · FREMONT, OHIO**
Charles was an **All-Pro** twice for the Packers.

4 — **JIM RINGO · ORANGE, NEW JERSEY**
Jim Ringo was a great blocker and an even better leader.

5 — **JAN STENERUD · FETSUND, NORWAY**
In 1981, Jan made 22 of 24 field goal attempts for Green Bay.

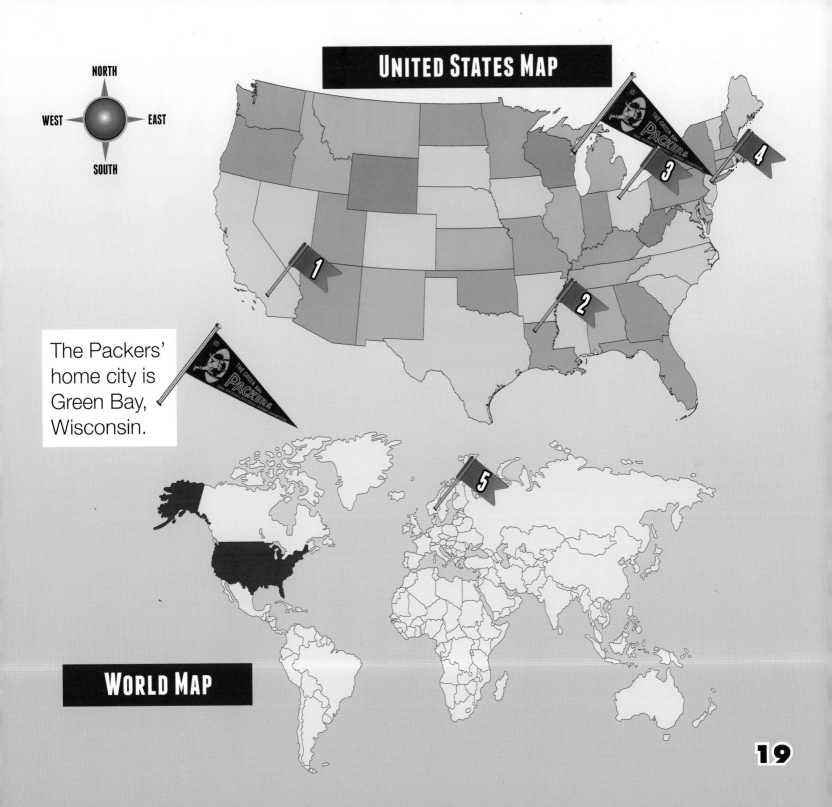

UNITED STATES MAP

NORTH

WEST — EAST

SOUTH

The Packers' home city is Green Bay, Wisconsin.

WORLD MAP

Jordy Nelson wears the Packers' home uniform.

Football teams wear different uniforms for home and away games. The main colors of the Packers are dark green and gold. In their early years, they wore blue and yellow uniforms.

Clay Matthews wears the Packers' away uniform.

The Packers' helmet is one of the most famous in football. It is gold with a white letter G on each side. The team began using this design in 1961.

WE WON!

Green Bay is known as "Titletown USA." The Packers won the NFL championship in 1929, 1930, and 1931. In the 1960s, coach **Vince Lombardi** led them to five more. The Packers finished the 2010 season by winning the team's 13th championship.

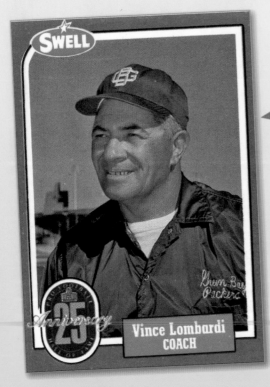

SWELL

Vince Lombardi
COACH

RECORD BOOK

These Packers set team records.

TOUCHDOWN PASSES	RECORD
Season: Aaron Rodgers (2011)	45
Career: Brett Favre	442

TOUCHDOWN CATCHES	RECORD
Season: Sterling Sharpe (1994)	18
Career: Don Hutson	99

RUSHING YARDS	RECORD
Season: **Ahman Green** (2003)	1,883
Career: Ahman Green	8,322

ANSWERS FOR THE BIG PICTURE
#71 changed to #77, #12's right sleeve changed color, and the logo on #27's helmet disappeared.

ANSWER FOR TRUE AND FALSE
#2 is false. Aaron never had a show called "Mr. Rodgers' Neighborhood."

All-Pro
An honor given to the best NFL player at each position.

Interception
A pass caught by a defensive player.

Pro Bowl
The NFL's annual all-star game.

Quarterback Sacks
Tackles of the quarterback that lose yardage.

Photos are on **BOLD** numbered pages.

ABOUT THE AUTHOR

Zack Burgess has been writing about sports for more than 20 years. He has lived all over the country and interviewed lots of All-Pro football players, including Brett Favre, Eddie George, Jerome Bettis, Shannon Sharpe, and Rich Gannon. Zack was the first African American beat writer to cover Major League Baseball when he worked for the *Kansas City Star*.

ABOUT THE PACKERS

Learn more at these websites:

www.packers.com • www.profootballhof.com

www.teamspiritextras.com/Overtime/html/packers.html